AMERICAN REVOLUTION
TECHNOLOGY

BY TAMMY GAGNE

CONTENT CONSULTANT
Abby Chandler
Associate Professor, History
University of Massachusetts, Lowell

Core Library

An Imprint of Abdo Publishing
abdopublishing.com

Cover image: US troops in the American Revolution
wore a variety of different uniforms.

abdopublishing.com

Published by Abdo Publishing, a division of ABDO, PO Box 398166, Minneapolis, Minnesota 55439. Copyright © 2018 by Abdo Consulting Group, Inc. International copyrights reserved in all countries. No part of this book may be reproduced in any form without written permission from the publisher. Core Library™ is a trademark and logo of Abdo Publishing.

Printed in the United States of America, North Mankato, Minnesota
032017
092017

Cover Photo: DeAgostini/Getty Images
Interior Photos: DeAgostini/Getty Images, 1; Hulton Archive/Getty Images, 4–5, 45; Barney Burstein/Corbis/VCG/Getty Images, 7; The Print Collector/Print Collector/Getty Images, 9; Universal History Archive/UIG/Getty Images, 10–11; Time Life Pictures/Mansell/The LIFE Picture Collection/Getty Images, 13; De Agostini/C. Balossini/Getty Images, 15; Jacqueline Larma/ AP Images, 16; North Wind Picture Archives, 18–19; Visions of America/UIG/Getty Images, 21; D. Trozzo/Alamy, 22; Kenneth Schulze/iStockphoto, 24; Interim Archives/Getty Images, 26–27; Red Line Editorial, 29; Dave Bartruff/Getty Images, 31; Stock Montage/Stock Montage/Getty Images, 34–35; Science Source, 36–37; John Trumbull, 40

Editor: Arnold Ringstad
Imprint Designer: Maggie Villaume
Series Design Direction: Nikki Farinella

Publisher's Cataloging-in-Publication Data

Names: Gagne, Tammy, author.
Title: American Revolutionary technology / by Tammy Gagne.
Description: Minneapolis, MN : Abdo Publishing, 2018. | Series: War technology
      | Includes bibliographical references and index.
Identifiers: LCCN 2017930438 | ISBN 9781532111884 (lib. bdg.) |
      ISBN 9781680789737 (ebook)
Subjects: LCSH: United States--History--Revolutionary War, 1775-1783--
          Technology--Juvenile literature. | Technology--United States--History--18th
          century--Juvenile literature.
      Classification: DDC 973.3--dc23
      LC record available at http://lccn.loc.gov/2017930438

CONTENTS

A FIGHT FOR INDEPENDENCE

As the sun rose, 77 colonial militiamen banded together. They stood on the town green in Lexington, Massachusetts. It was April 19, 1775. The men had weapons called muskets. Each militiaman carried powder and musket balls. Approximately 700 British troops soon arrived. They told the colonists to put down their weapons. The militia's commander knew his men were outnumbered. He was ready to back down. Suddenly someone fired a weapon.

No one knows who fired that first shot. But it marked the beginning of a war.

The musket shots at Lexington became the first shots of the American Revolutionary War.

GETTING WEAPONS

Today soldiers receive weapons when they enlist. Modern armies often use the latest technology. But the colonists had few resources. They could not provide soldiers with the best weapons of the day. The Americans had to get weapons in other ways. Friendly iron foundry owners provided some equipment. Many militiamen used their own muskets.

The British troops fired shots into the crowd. The colonists returned fire. They wounded a single British soldier. Eight militiamen were killed. Another nine were injured. The American Revolutionary War (1775–1783) had begun.

FROM COLONISTS TO REBELS

Great Britain sent its first colonists to North America in 1607. This first settlement was called Jamestown. The area around it would later become Virginia. Relations between the colonies and Great Britain became strained in the 1700s. Great Britain and France fought in North America in the French and Indian War (1754–1763). To pay its war debts, Great Britain raised taxes. This made the colonists angry. They had no representatives in the

A colonial printing of an image of the Boston Massacre helped spread outrage over the event.

British government. They paid taxes, but no one was casting votes on their behalf.

The colonists demanded representation. They were ignored. Many began staging protests. Some of this activity happened in Boston, Massachusetts. In 1770, British soldiers fired their muskets upon colonists there. They killed five people. This event was known as the Boston Massacre. It helped turn colonists against the British. Another incident happened in 1773. It is known as the Boston Tea Party. Colonists dumped British tea into Boston Harbor.

In 1774 the colonists organized the Continental Congress. This group included George Washington, John Adams, and other colonists. They met in Philadelphia, Pennsylvania. The delegates expressed anger. Still, Great Britain refused to meet their demands.

PERSPECTIVES

TAKING AWAY TECHNOLOGY

After the events at Lexington, the British troops traveled to the nearby town of Concord. They were searching for military supplies. They hoped that taking away the colonists' weapons would prevent the rebellion. The British soldiers destroyed artillery pieces. They even tossed ammunition into nearby ponds. Despite the losses, many colonists remained determined to fight for independence.

Following the shooting at Lexington, more militiamen joined the cause. Later that day, they clashed with British troops in Concord, Massachusetts. By the end of the day, the militia had lost approximately 90 men. They had killed or wounded about 250 British troops. In 1775

The primary weapons of the war were handheld firearms and larger artillery pieces.

the Continental Congress formed the Continental Army to fight the British.

The American Revolution marked a turning point in world history. The military technology of the time helped make the American victory possible. New firearm designs, deadly artillery weapons, and the use of codes and spies had strong influences on future wars.

REVOLUTIONARY FIREARMS

The most common firearm of the war was the flintlock musket. This weapon is sometimes called a long smoothbore gun. The inside of its barrel is smooth rather than grooved. Soldiers held muskets with both hands. They fired these weapons from the shoulder. The end of a musket often held a bayonet. This knife-like attachment was used in close combat.

The biggest downfall of the musket was that it was not accurate past 100 yards (91 m). This meant troops had to get close to each other. Once the enemy was within range, a

Large muskets with bayonets on the end were typical among Revolutionary War soldiers.

A NEW TYPE OF MUSKET

Matchlock muskets had been around for more than three centuries when the American Revolution began. A matchlock musket had a small gunpowder pan on it. To fire the gun, a soldier lowered a match to ignite the powder. Matchlocks were unreliable. They would misfire approximately half the time. Flintlock muskets were more reliable. They did not require the user to light the gunpowder by hand. Instead, they used flint to create sparks. These sparks ignited the powder. This saved time and effort when firing. Still, soldiers needed to keep sharp edges on their flint. Both matchlocks and flintlocks were hard to fire in wet conditions.

group of soldiers fired their muskets all at once. This mass firing was called a volley. The soldiers then charged with their bayonets.

One important musket was the British land pattern musket. This weapon was nicknamed the Brown Bess. The weapon was in service from 1722 into the 1860s. British soldiers carried Brown Bess muskets. Continental soldiers used them when they could capture the guns from their enemies.

THE BROWN BESS

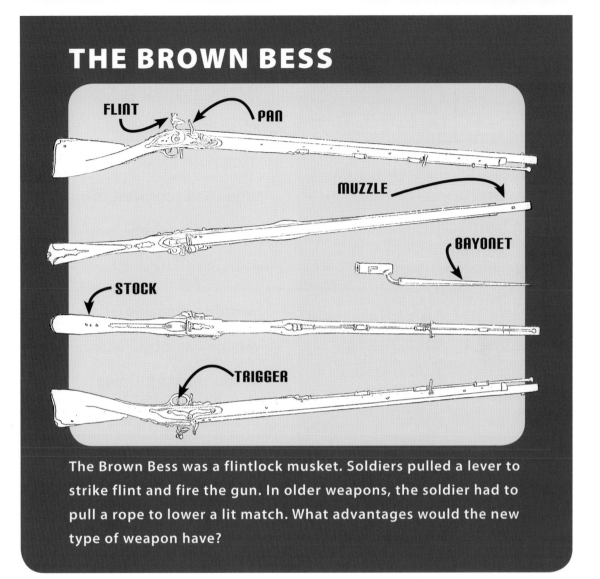

FLINT PAN MUZZLE BAYONET STOCK TRIGGER

The Brown Bess was a flintlock musket. Soldiers pulled a lever to strike flint and fire the gun. In older weapons, the soldier had to pull a rope to lower a lit match. What advantages would the new type of weapon have?

RIFLES

Unlike muskets, rifles did not have smooth barrels. Gun makers cut spiraling grooves into them. These grooves are known as rifling. They spin the bullet as it leaves the gun. This makes the bullet's flight more

According to the *Journal of the American Revolution*, a private in the Continental Army once saw a musket ball travel more than half a mile (0.8 km). His regiment spotted British soldiers on some rocks. A British soldier fired on them. However, they seemed far out of range. One Continental Army soldier fired back. To the surprise of the American troops, the British soldier dropped. The Americans thought the soldier was playing dead as a joke. But when morning came, his body was in the same spot. It is unclear what type of weapon the Continental soldier used.

stable, increasing accuracy. The war's rifles had about three times the range of the average musket.

Despite its benefits, the rifle was not as popular as the musket. Rifles had a slower rate of fire. They also could not hold bayonets. These problems made rifles a poor choice for soldiers facing large armies.

Weapons often left large clouds of smoke when fired, revealing the position of the soldier.

Pistols used during the American Revolution are now carefully preserved in museums.

PISTOLS

Pistols are shorter than muskets and rifles. They are fired with one hand. The pistols of the Revolutionary War were only accurate at close range. They were rare on the battlefield. Officers, mounted troops, and sailors used them most often.

STRAIGHT TO THE
SOURCE

New technology can sometimes be unreliable at first. Historian Thomas Fleming discussed an example of this in the Ferguson repeating rifle:

> *It was a weapon that could have won the war for the British, but their bureaucracy was too hidebound to perceive this. Major Patrick Ferguson managed to persuade the royal ordinance works to produce 100 copies of the gun, which was a breech loader and could fire seven times without reloading. Modern replicas have fired sixty times without jamming. It was deadly at 200–300 yards [183–274 m], far better than an ordinary musket. . . . But it was difficult to produce and broke down during combat if the breech was not frequently lubricated. Howe disbanded the Ferguson unit and stored the guns in New York. Ferguson was killed at the Battle of Kings Mountain and the gun was forgotten.*

> Source: "Most Famous Weapon?" *Journal of the American Revolution*. Journal of the American Revolution, July 16, 2016. Web. Accessed December 20, 2016.

Consider Your Audience

Read the passage above closely. Write a blog post about this information for a new audience, such as your classmates. How does your post differ from the original text, and why?

ARTILLERY: THE BIG GUNS

Artillery weapons were key to victory in the American Revolution. Troops used three major types: cannons, mortars, and howitzers. They allowed soldiers to strike the enemy from great distances. These large weapons could significantly alter the balance of power. Placing artillery around a besieged city could intimidate troops into surrendering.

CANNONS

Like muskets, the war's cannons had smooth barrels. But the barrels were much bigger than those of firearms. The cannons themselves were usually cast in either iron or bronze.

Artillery pieces were used against troops, buildings, and ships.

Their great weight meant each one needed a crew of several men.

To fire a cannon, soldiers would first insert a cartridge into its front opening. This opening is called a muzzle. The cartridge was paper or cloth filled with gunpowder. Next the soldiers placed a cannonball into the muzzle. They then put gunpowder into a tube that led to the cartridge. Soldiers

Cannons are sometimes fired at events reenacting the Revolutionary War. Participants use accurate uniforms and equipment.

lit this gunpowder. The flame traveled to the cartridge, which exploded. This launched the cannonball out at high speed. The force of the shot pushed the weapon backward. Crew members had to move it back into place to fire again.

MORTARS

Mortars were used for firing high shots over short ranges. The shells dropped on the enemy from above. The mortars used in the war looked a bit like thicker, shorter cannons.

TRANSPORTING WEAPONRY

One of the hardest parts of using artillery was getting it into place. Continental Army officer Henry Knox built sleds to transport artillery from New York to Boston. The Americans laid siege to Boston in 1776. To threaten the city, Knox and his soldiers moved cannons, howitzers, and mortars there. They placed the weapons on the hills surrounding Boston Harbor. This arsenal helped the colonists take the city from the British. The British commander, General William Howe, abandoned Boston after he saw the artillery.

Mortars fired large shells at steep angles.

As with handheld weapons, firing cannons from the Revolutionary War era can produce a great deal of smoke.

But they differed from regular cannons in a few ways. Mortars had a chambered design. This meant they had a hollow space near the back. This chamber was for the gunpowder. The mortar shell would sit on a ledge above this chamber. Keeping the weight of the shell off the powder was important. Its weight could prevent the powder from igniting or make the weapon fire accidentally during loading. Mortars also gave soldiers the ability to fire bombs. These were shells filled with gunpowder. They exploded when hitting the target.

HOWITZERS

Howitzers looked like cannons with shorter barrels. But they were much lighter in weight. Like mortars, they had chambers. The howitzer offered soldiers some of the best features of both cannons and mortars.

One of the biggest advantages of the howitzer was that it could fire either a solid cannonball or a bomb. A howitzer could also be fired at a flat angle or on a high arc. This let the crew hit targets head-on or from above.

EXPLORE ONLINE

Chapter Three discusses artillery weapons used in the American Revolution. The website below goes into more detail on this topic. How is the information from the website the same as the information in Chapter Three? What new information did you learn from the website?

REVOLUTIONARY WAR ARTILLERY
abdocorelibrary.com/american-revolution-tech

SUPPORT TECHNOLOGY

Weapons are not all that soldiers need. Both sides must create strategies. Then they must communicate the plans to their troops. Finally, they need to tend to their wounded. Technology plays a big part in these important goals.

COMMUNICATION TECHNOLOGY

Letters and spoken messages were the main forms of communication during the war. Messengers traveled on horseback to deliver news. Paul Revere made one of these famous journeys. Before the battles at Lexington and

Riders on horseback were among the fastest means of communication during the American Revolution.

Concord, he rode to warn colonists that the British were coming. William Dawes and Samuel Prescott also rode into the countryside that night.

Letters were more private than spoken words. But written messages could be read by anyone. By writing messages in code, armies could communicate with less risk.

Few soldiers knew much about codes at the start of the American Revolution. But Continental general Nathanael Greene had a background as a merchant. Members of this profession often used codes to keep their communications secret. Greene taught

THE PRINTING PRESS

Printing presses had important effects on the war. By the 1760s, many colonial towns had printing presses. Publishers created newspapers and pamphlets about the war. Presses made copies of engraved images. An engraved drawing of the Boston Massacre was widely distributed soon after the event. The image was meant to draw more people to the revolutionary cause.

CODED MESSAGES

711 683 38 72 635 5 106 282 737

5: and	**282:** in	**683:** will
38: attack	**332:** infection	**709:** yesterday
72: British	**489:** prison	**711:** General George Washington
106: cannon	**506:** protect	**712:** General Clinton
255: horse	**635:** troops	**737:** New Jersey

George Washington ordered the creation of a spy group in 1778. It was known as the Culper Spy Ring. The group used a code book that used numbers to stand for particular words. Spies could communicate with each other safely using these codes. Above is a sample of coded text, along with the key to decode the message. What does the coded message say? What are the strengths and weaknesses of this type of code?

his soldiers code writing. The cipher used numbers in place of words. Each number matched a word in a codebook owned by both parties.

SPY TECHNOLOGY

The first American spy ring was the Mercereau spy ring. It operated in New York and New Jersey.

Spies sometimes took jobs in mail delivery. They would stop along their routes to let army leaders read certain letters.

While this did not involve much technology, covering a spy's tracks did. Letter writers often used wax seals on their letters. Spies had to copy these seals. This let them reseal opened letters. Then they could deliver the letters as usual.

MILITARY MEDICAL CARE

Many soldiers were injured in Revolutionary War battles. Those who were treated successfully could go on to fight another day. Infected wounds posed a major threat. A battlefield was often a dirty environment. It was the perfect breeding ground for infections.

Illness was also a big concern. Several diseases were widespread. Smallpox was one of the deadliest. One of the biggest advances of the time was

A Revolutionary War reenactor stands with a variety of medical tools used during the war.

A PIONEER OF ARMY MEDICINE

Compared to today's standards, medical care during the American Revolution was basic. Neither army offered its soldiers much medical training. When someone was seriously injured, other soldiers would do their best to care for him. But many times they were little help. A Continental Army surgeon named John Jones introduced lifesaving techniques. In 1775 he wrote an army medical manual. Regular soldiers could use it to help the wounded.

inoculation. In this process, a person would be given a mild form of smallpox. His or her immune system would learn how to fight the disease. This would enable it to fight off smallpox in the future. George Washington ordered his soldiers to get inoculated in 1777. This action likely saved many lives.

STRAIGHT TO THE
SOURCE

Historian John A. Nagy compared Revolutionary War spy techniques with those used today:

The modern intelligence world still uses most of the intelligence methods from the American Revolution but with more sophistication in its encryption. During the American Revolution they used dead drops where a message is left at a location and the intended agent comes and picks it up. Robert Hanson, the FBI agent who was spying for the Russians, left his messages under a wooden bridge in Vienna, Virginia. When he was caught in 2001, he reportedly used the dead drop twenty times. In the 1950s a Russian spy in New York City used a hollowed out coin to hide messages. Modern British spies were alleged to have used an electronic rock as a receiver and transmitter of messages.

Source: "An Interview with John Nagy." *Mount Vernon*. Mount Vernon Ladies' Association, n.d. Web. January 24, 2017.

What's the Big Idea?
Take a close look at this passage. How does Nagy connect Revolutionary War spying with today's methods? How has technology changed the art of spying?

TECHNOLOGY ON THE WATER

The Revolutionary War was fought in North America. British reinforcements were far away. They had to travel by sea from Great Britain. This made ships important to the war. Additionally, many key battles were fought near the coast. Naval technology became an important factor for both sides.

BUILDING WAR SHIPS

In 1775, the Continental Congress formed the Continental Navy. The meeting, which included John Adams, was a productive one. The Continental Congress ordered colonial shipbuilders to construct 13 frigates.

The Continental Navy was small, but it had the advantage of operating near friendly shores.

During naval battles, ships often got close enough for crews to fire guns at individual enemy sailors.

Shipbuilding had been an important industry in the colonies since the 1600s. But building these ships would take time. While they waited for the new vessels, members of the new Continental Navy used converted merchant ships instead. Most of the navy's ships ended up being taken in battle by Britain's more experienced Royal Navy.

SINKING THE ENEMY

The Continental Navy's warships were equipped with naval weapons. The guns and artillery were similar to those used by land soldiers. The biggest difference was that naval crews did not move artillery weapons. They were attached to specific spots on the ship.

The Continental Navy used technology to improve the effectiveness of their artillery. Sailors often fired pairs of cannonballs chained together. These were known as chain shot. The cannonballs spun after leaving the muzzle. Chain shot could take down the masts and rigging of an enemy ship. This would make it impossible for the ship to steer.

Soldiers used hot shot to make their cannons more powerful. First they would heat a cannonball. They would then place wet rags inside the cannon's barrel. This kept the red-hot ball separate from the gunpowder. Finally, they would fire the cannon. The ball would set its target ablaze. The luckiest shots hit the enemy ship's gunpowder storage. This could cause a huge explosion. Soldiers sank a British ship at Yorktown in 1781 using this method.

THE END OF THE WAR

The Continental Army began fighting at a disadvantage. The army did not even exist until after the fighting at Lexington and Concord. Troops were still learning to work together as the battles were happening. The colonists had important help from the French. The French sent troops, ships, and supplies.

At the Yorktown surrender, Washington's second-in-command, Benjamin Lincoln, accepted a sword from a British representative. The British commander, Lord Cornwallis, refused to attend.

But the Americans still had limited resources compared to the British.

Despite all these shortcomings, the Continental Army was dedicated to winning the war. The soldiers combined their limited technology with their passion for the cause. In October 1781, the Continental Army and French troops surrounded British troops at Yorktown, Virginia. The British surrendered. This victory marked the end of the Revolutionary War. Two years later, the Treaty of Paris made the war's end official. The colonists had won their independence. From weapons to ships to codes, they had used a variety of technologies in their struggle to create a new nation.

FURTHER EVIDENCE

Chapter Five discusses naval technology used during the American Revolution. What is the main idea of this chapter? What key evidence supports this idea? Take a look at the website below. Find information from the site that supports the main idea of this chapter. Does the information support an existing piece of evidence in the chapter, or does it add new evidence?

THE RISE OF THE AMERICAN NAVY 1775-1914

abdocorelibrary.com/american-revolution-tech

IMPORTANT
DATES

1722

The Brown Bess musket enters service with Great Britain.

1774

The colonists organize the Continental Congress.

1775

The Continental Congress orders shipbuilders to construct 13 new frigates for the navy.

1775

John Jones writes a military medical manual.

1775

Before the Battles of Lexington and Concord, Paul Revere rides on horseback on April 18 to warn the colonists that the British are coming.

1775

On April 19, colonists and British troops clash in Lexington.

1776

During the Siege of Boston, US troops bring artillery to the city and reclaim Boston from British troops.

1776

Esek Hopkins sails to the Bahamas to raid British supplies.

1776

Margaret Cochran Corbin becomes the first woman to join Revolutionary War combat.

1777

George Washington orders his troops to get inoculated against smallpox.

1781

At the Battle of Yorktown, artillery troops sink a British ship with hot shot.

1781

In October the British surrender to US forces at Yorktown, Virginia.

STOP AND
THINK

Tell the Tale

Chapter One of this book discusses the reasons the colonists went to war for their independence from Great Britain. Imagine that you are living in one of the colonies before the American Revolution began. Write 200 words about your experience. How do you feel about paying taxes without someone representing you in government? Do you think you might have taken part in a protest such as the Boston Tea Party?

Another View

This book discusses the technology used in the American Revolution. As you know, every source is different. Ask an adult to help you find another source about this topic. Write a short essay comparing and contrasting the new source's point of view with that of this book's author. What point does each author make? How are they the same? How are they different?

Take a Stand

This book discusses the use of firearms in the American Revolution. Many Continental soldiers used their own muskets. Do you think using these personal weapons helped the Continental Army win the war? Write a paragraph about your opinion. Use evidence to support your answer.

Say What?

Reading a book about war technology can involve learning new vocabulary. Find five words in this book that you had not seen before. Use the glossary or a dictionary to find their definitions. Next, write the meanings in your own words and use each word in a new sentence.

GLOSSARY

arsenal
a collection of weapons

cipher
a message written in code
in which various symbols or
letters stand for other letters

delegate
a person sent to a meeting
to represent others

foundry
a place where metal tools
are created

frigate
a fast warship with weapons
on one or two decks

militiamen
a group of citizens who
come together to create a
military force

pension
a sum of money paid to a
person after retirement

provisions
a stock of supplies

LEARN MORE

Books

Kjelle, Marylou Morano. *The Boston Massacre.* Minneapolis, MN: Abdo Publishing, 2013.

Murphy, Jim. *The Crossing: How George Washington Saved the American Revolution.* New York: Scholastic, 2016.

Murray, Stuart. *The American Revolution.* New York: DK Publishing, 2015.

Websites

To learn more about War Technology, visit **abdobooklinks.com**. These links are routinely monitored and updated to provide the most current information available.

Visit **abdocorelibrary.com** for free additional tools for teachers and students.

INDEX

About the Author

Tammy Gagne has written dozens of books for both adults and children. Her recent titles include *Incredible Military Weapons* and *Military Dogs*. She lives in northern New England with her husband, son, and pets.